AMERICAN CIVIL RIGHTS LEADERS

The *Collective Biographies* Series

Collective Biographies

AMERICAN CIVIL RIGHTS LEADERS

Rod Harmon

Enslow Publishers, Inc.

40 Industrial Road	PO Box 38
Box 398	Aldershot
Berkeley Heights, NJ 07922	Hants GU12 6BP
USA	UK

http://www.enslow.com

Library of Congress Cataloging-in-Publication Data

Harmon, Rod.
American civil rights leaders / by Rod Harmon.
    p. cm. — (Collective biographies)
Includes bibliographical references and index.
Summary: Profiles prominent men and women of the civil rights movement,
including Charles Houston, Ella Baker, Thurgood Marshall, Rosa Parks,
Fannie Lou Hamer, Malcolm X, Martin Luther King, Jr., Andrew Young,
Julian Bond, and Jesse Jackson.
    ISBN 0-7660-1381-2
    1. Afro-American civil rights workers—Biography—Juvenile literature.
2. Afro-American political activists—Biography—Juvenile literature.
3. Afro-Americans—Civil rights—History—20th century—Juvenile
literature. 4. Civil rights movements—United States—History—20th
century—Juvenile literature. 5. United States—Race
relations—Juvenile literature. [1. Civil rights workers. 2. Political
activists. 3. Afro-Americans—Civil rights—History—20th century.
4. Civil rights movements—History—20th century. 5. Race relations.
6. Afro-Americans—Biography.] I. Title. II. Series.
    E185.96 .H334   2000
    323.1'196073'0922—dc21
                                                    00-008514

Printed in the United States of America

10 9 8 7 6 5 4 3 2 1

To Our Readers:
All Internet addresses in this book were active and appropriate when we went to press.
Any comments or suggestions can be sent by e-mail to Comments@enslow.com or to
the address on the back cover.

Every effort has been made to locate all copyright holders of material used in this
book. If any errors or omissions have occurred, corrections will be made in future
editions of this book.

Illustration Credits: Illustrations: Alabama Department of Archives and
History, p. 69; AP/World Wide Photos, pp. 41, 52; Birmingham Public
Library, p. 77; Boston University, p. 67; Jackson for President, p. 93;
Johnson Publishing Company, Inc., p. 27; Library of Congress, pp. 18, 23,
44, 58, 61, 74, 80, 89; Moorland Spingarn Research Center, p. 14; National
Archives, pp. 31, 36; Schomberg Center for Research in Black Culture, The
New York Public Library, Astor, Lenox and Tilden Foundations, pp. 49, 85;
Special Collections and Archives, W.E.B. Du Bois Library, University of
Massachusetts Amherst, p. 9.

Cover Illustration: Johnson Publishing Company, Inc.

Contents

Preface

In 1863, President Abraham Lincoln signed the Emancipation Proclamation. Issued in the middle of the Civil War, it signaled the first step toward the end of slavery and gave African Americans hope that they would at last be given the same rights as whites.

It seemed those hopes would be realized. When the Civil War ended in 1865, the antislavery North had won. Reconstruction was the period from the end of the Civil War until 1876, when the federal government tried to rebuild the South and protect the rights of former slaves there. In the next five years the United States Congress passed three amendments and many important pieces of civil rights legislation. The Thirteenth Amendment, passed in 1865, abolished slavery. The Fourteenth Amendment, passed in 1866, gave blacks social and civil rights, like the right to own property and to testify in court. The Fifteenth Amendment, passed in 1870, gave blacks the right to vote.

But it did not take long for the South to find new ways to deny African Americans the rights guaranteed by Congress. When Reconstruction ended in 1876, the federal government stopped protecting the rights of southern blacks. Many southern states passed new laws to restrict the freedom of African Americans. Some new laws tried to keep blacks from voting, including having to pay a tax or to pass a literacy test to vote. Often white government officials would only make blacks pass these tests. By the beginning of the twentieth century, southern states also enacted "Jim Crow" laws that made it illegal for blacks and whites to share things like drinking fountains, restrooms, theaters, lunch counters, and schools. This separation was known as segregation.

In 1896, the United States Supreme Court ruled segregation was legal in the *Plessy* v. *Ferguson* case. Homer Plessy had sued a Louisiana railroad company that refused to let him sit in a "whites-only" rail car. Plessy looked white, but had a black great-grandmother. The Supreme Court said segregation was constitutional as long as "separate but equal" facilities were available to both whites and blacks.

The Supreme Court's ruling provided southern states with an excuse to deny African Americans their civil rights—the rights guaranteed under the Constitution. While there were separate facilities for blacks and whites, they were usually far from equal. This inequality extended into every aspect of African-American life. Blacks were prevented from voting, running for office, obtaining good jobs, living where they wanted, and even eating and drinking where they chose. Those who complained or fought back lost their jobs, had their houses burned, or were killed.

Despite these difficulties, African Americans never stopped demanding equality and civil rights.

Beginning in 1909, the National Association for the Advancement of Colored People (NAACP) and its leading spokesman, W. E. B. Du Bois, fought for equality for African Americans. The NAACP fought for new federal laws to protect African Americans from violence and discrimination and tried to challenge southern laws that discriminated against African Americans.

On May 17, 1954, the walls of legalized segregation began to tumble down. In a case called *Brown* v. *Board of Education of Topeka* (Kansas), the Supreme Court ruled that segregation in public schools was illegal. In the *Brown* decision, the Supreme Court reversed the earlier *Plessy* v. *Ferguson* case and argued that separate was not equal.

From 1954 to 1965 and beyond, many African Americans seized the momentum started by the *Brown* case to end segregation and Jim Crow laws once and for all. They would not shop at businesses that discriminated against blacks. They organized voter registration drives. They refused to move from whites-only lunch counters until they were served. They marched through southern towns that denied African Americans their rights.

The road to civil rights was hard. Harassment, violence and even death threatened civil rights activists every day of their lives. But they did not give up. They would settle for nothing less than what the United States Constitution says every American deserves: equality.

In 1905 a number of African-American leaders, including W. E. B. Du Bois (second row, second from right), met at Niagara Falls, Canada, to fight racial discrimination. In 1909 the NAACP adopted many of the ideas of the "Niagara Movement."

This book is about some of the key players in the civil rights movement. Some of them are well known, like Thurgood Marshall, the chief lawyer in the *Brown* case who became a Supreme Court justice; Malcolm X, the Nation of Islam minister who inspired blacks to fight for their rights; Jesse Jackson, the first African American to make a serious bid for the presidency; and Martin Luther King, Jr., a Baptist minister whose name has become almost as one with the words *civil rights*.

There are also people who are not well known but whose battles were just as important to the civil rights movement. Charles Houston's early legal victories paved the way for the *Brown* decision; Fannie Lou Hamer challenged segregation at the 1964 Democratic Party convention; and Andrew Young went on to become one of the first African Americans elected to Congress in the 1900s. Each of these men and women played significant roles in the success of the civil rights movement.

The leaders of the civil rights movement had a dream that America would one day be the land of hope for all Americans, not just a few. The struggle continues to this day, but their work helped lay the tracks for a train that once started, cannot stop. These are their stories.

1

Charles Houston
(1895–1950)

Lawsuits mean little unless supported by public opinion," Charles Houston once wrote. "Nobody needs to explain to [an African American] the difference between law in books and the law in action."[1] As a lawyer for the National Association for the Advancement of Colored People (NAACP), Charles Houston understood that difference very well. Houston dedicated his life to making the reality fit the law and wipe out the unequal treatment of blacks. Although his name is not very well known, he laid the legal groundwork for the civil rights movement.[2]

Charles Hamilton Houston was born September 3, 1895. He was the only son of William and Mary Houston. His family had a long history of struggling for civil rights. His grandfather, Thomas Jefferson Houston, was a slave who escaped to freedom and helped other slaves escape. His father was a lawyer and a part-time instructor at the Howard University School of Law in Washington, D.C. From an early age, Charles's parents stressed the importance of a good education.

Charles graduated at age sixteen from M Street High School in Washington. At the time, it was one of the best African-American schools in the nation. He got a scholarship to Amherst College in Massachusetts, where he was the only black student. After graduating from Amherst in 1915, he joined his father as a part-time faculty member at Howard, teaching English. Houston immediately added a new course to the English curriculum: African-American literature.

In 1917, the United States entered World War I, and Houston faced the possibility of being drafted. Like many African Americans, he was uncomfortable fighting for a country that treated African Americans as second-class citizens. At the time, black soldiers were separated from white soldiers and commanded by white officers. Houston and other Howard University faculty members and students petitioned the federal government to establish a black officers' training camp. The government agreed, and in June 1917, Houston began his training as an officer. He became a first lieutenant in October 1917.

Houston served as a judge advocate in the army and handled cases involving African-American soldiers. A judge advocate investigates and prosecutes military court-martial cases. Houston quickly discovered that racism existed in the military judicial system. African Americans were almost always presumed guilty, and their sentences were usually much harsher than those of white soldiers who had committed the same crimes.

The unequal treatment inspired Houston to become a lawyer and fight for civil rights. "I made up my mind that I would never get caught again without knowing something about my rights," Houston later wrote. "If luck was with me, and I got through this war, I would study law and use my time fighting for men who could not strike back."[3]

World War I ended before Houston saw any fighting. He then enrolled in Harvard University Law School in Cambridge, Massachusetts. Once again, he was an outstanding student, and, based on his grades, was the first African American to serve on the editorial board of the prestigious *Harvard Law Review*. He received his law degree in 1922. Houston continued his education on a scholarship, earned a doctoral degree in law from Harvard in 1923, and studied in Spain for several months.

In 1924, Houston married his college sweetheart, Margaret Gladys Moran, and started working for his father's law practice. As a lawyer, Houston represented many poor African Americans who could

Charles Houston

barely pay him. Keeping with the vow he made while in the military, Houston helped those who could not help themselves. He looked with disdain upon black lawyers who practiced law mainly for money. Such lawyers did not respond to "civic or racial matters which do not touch directly upon their own personal interests," Houston believed.[4]

Houston also began teaching at Howard again, this time in the university's law school. In 1929, he was appointed vice dean of the law school. He strengthened the curriculum and helped the school gain accreditation from the American Bar Association. This made it much easier for Howard University Law School to attract good students—both black and white.

Houston demanded excellence from his students. He believed African-American lawyers had to be "social engineers." Social engineers, he said, were lawyers who had an exhaustive knowledge of the United States Constitution and could attack the problems of society through the courts.[5] One of his students was Thurgood Marshall, who would later become a leading force in the civil rights movement and a Supreme Court justice.

Marshall remembered the important influence Houston had on many of his students. "[Houston] used to tell us that doctors could bury their mistakes, but lawyers couldn't," Marshall said many years later. "And he'd drive home to us that we would be competing not only with white lawyers but really well-trained white lawyers, so there was not any point in crying in our beer about being [African Americans]. . . . He made it clear to all of us that when we were done, we were expected to go out and do something with our lives."[6]

In 1935, Houston helped the NAACP start a legal campaign against the separation of races in public schools. Throughout the country, especially in the South, white schools had more money, better supplies and better facilities than African-American schools. The inequality meant African Americans did not get the education necessary to compete on equal footing. Houston took a leave of absence from Howard to become the NAACP's chief legal counsel, and filmed conditions at black schools throughout the South to help make a case against segregation.

Houston's plan was to start at the professional school level and work his way down to colleges, then high schools, and finally elementary schools. He chose to begin with professional schools because he felt white people would be less threatened by integrating these schools. In 1935, Thurgood Marshall, now a lawyer with his own practice in Baltimore, Maryland, told Houston about Donald Gaines Murray, an African American who had been denied admission to the University of Maryland's law school based on his race. The case became Houston's launching pad for ending segregation.[7]

Houston and Marshall worked together on the case, arguing that Murray was denied a "separate but equal" opportunity that the Supreme Court had required in *Plessy* v. *Ferguson.* In that case, the court ruled it was acceptable to have separate facilities for whites and blacks as long as they were equal.

Houston's goal was to show that the University of Maryland was not providing a separate law school for Murray. "It is plain that the State of Maryland has not offered [Murray] the equivalent of the opportunities and advantages which he would have in studying law in the School of Law of the University of Maryland," Houston and Marshall wrote in a legal brief. The court agreed and ruled that the university must admit Murray. It was one of the first steps toward ending segregation.[8]

Houston was happy with the decision. Still, his long-term goal was not just to require schools to honor the "separate but equal" rule. Houston wanted the Supreme Court to rule segregation unconstitutional. He persuaded Marshall to work for the NAACP full time, and they traveled the South together, gathering evidence of the shabby conditions African-American students had to endure.

Houston focused almost all of his attention on his legal work. His marriage suffered as a result, and he and Margaret were divorced in 1937. Later that same year, he married his secretary, Henrietta Williams. The couple later had a son, Charles Hamilton Houston, Jr.

In 1938, Houston successfully argued another case before the Supreme Court that resulted in the

University of Missouri opening its doors to an African-American law student. Recognizing a chance to end segregation once and for all, in 1939 the NAACP established the NAACP Legal Defense Fund to fight civil rights battles in the courtroom.

Houston resigned as the NAACP's chief counsel in 1938 to join his father's law practice, and was replaced by Marshall. Still, Houston continued to assist the NAACP as a member of its National Legal Committee. Houston helped the organization prepare its civil rights cases, including the case that would finally prove that separate was unequal: *Brown* v. *Board of Education of Topeka* (Kansas).

On April 22, 1950, at the age of 54, Charles Houston died from heart disease. Just four years later, on May 17, 1954, the Supreme Court ruled in the *Brown* case that segregation in all schools

In this photograph, Walter White (left), NAACP Executive Secretary, poses with Houston (second from left) and other NAACP Legal Defense Fund lawyers.

was unconstitutional. Houston's dream was finally realized.

"When *Brown v. the Board of Education of Topeka* was being argued in the Supreme Court," Marshall later said of Houston's legacy, "there were some two dozen lawyers on the side of [African Americans] fighting for their schools . . . of those lawyers, only two had not been touched by Charlie Houston. That man was the engineer of all of it."[9]

2

Ella Baker
(1903–1986)

Of all the leaders in the civil rights movement, no one avoided the spotlight more than Ella Baker. She preferred playing a behind-the-scenes role to having her name in the newspapers. Working with more than fifty organizations and coalitions over her lifetime, Baker helped shape some of the most important events in civil rights history.[1]

Ella Josephine Baker was born in Norfork, Virginia, on December 13, 1903, the second of three children. Her parents, Blake and Georgianna Ross Baker, were both children of former slaves. When Ella was seven, the family moved to Littleton, North Carolina. Her mother became deeply involved in the community and would often feed the hungry, wash clothes and midwife for needy women giving birth.

Ella was proud of this family tradition of helping others. "If you share your food with people, you share your lives with people," she would often say.[2]

When Baker was fifteen, her parents sent her to Shaw Boarding School, an all-black school in Raleigh, North Carolina. In 1927, she graduated with a Bachelor of Arts degree from Shaw University, a college affiliated with the boarding school, and moved to New York City. In New York, Baker lived in Harlem, where a growing African-American community thrived. Authors, musicians, and political activists made Harlem the center of what was called the Harlem Renaissance.

Then, in 1929, the United States plunged into the Great Depression. The Great Depression was one of the worst economic periods in American history. People went hungry and suffered because work was hard to find—especially for African Americans. Disturbed by the harsh conditions she saw in the black community of Harlem, Baker became involved in politics. In 1931, she became the first national director of the newly formed Young Negroes Cooperative League (YNCL), a group that fought for rights in the schools and the workplace. Baker soon became involved in recruitment efforts, and within one year, the YNCL had more than 400 members.[3]

In 1937, Baker became an assistant project director for the Work Projects Administration, a government program that provided work and taught job skills to the poor. Baker believed it was her job to develop grassroots leaders by giving them independence to express their ideas.

Baker believed that African Americans could not rely on others for help. They had to do it for themselves. "The [African American] must quit looking for a savior and work to save himself and wake up others," she said. "There is no salvation except through yourselves."[4]

Independence was very important to Baker. In 1940, when Baker married her college sweetheart, T. J. Roberts, nearly all women took their husbands' last name. Baker did not. She felt strongly about maintaining her personal identity.[5]

Also in 1940, Baker joined the National Association for the Advancement of Colored People (NAACP) as a field secretary. She became the NAACP's director of branches three years later. Both jobs required that she travel throughout the country recruiting and training people in local NAACP chapters. She developed a strong network of civil rights contacts that would become invaluable during the 1950s and 1960s.

By 1946, Baker was frustrated with the leadership of the NAACP. She felt that too much power was given to a few people and not enough to the local branches. Baker also believed that women were unfairly excluded from decision-making. She resigned, but continued to serve as a volunteer. Baker also wanted to spend more time raising her nine-year-old niece, Jacqueline. Jacqueline's mother,

Ella Baker

Baker's sister, was not prepared to raise a child, so Georgianna Ross Baker, Jacqueline's grandmother, had taken her when she was an infant. By 1946, Baker felt that Georgianna Baker was getting too old to take care of the child, so she assumed custody.

During the late 1940s and early 1950s, Baker continued to be politically active. She was especially interested in ending segregation. In 1955, she plunged into a bus boycott in Montgomery, Alabama. It had started because an African-American woman, Rosa Parks, had refused to give up her seat to a white man on a city bus and was arrested. In protest, the African-American citizens of Montgomery banded together under the leadership of Martin Luther King, Jr., and staged a boycott of the bus company until it ended the separation of blacks and whites.

Baker helped found an organization called In Friendship to raise funds for the boycott. When King and other ministers formed the Southern Christian Leadership Conference in 1957, Baker became the group's executive director. She organized voter registration drives and fund-raising efforts.

In February 1960, college students began staging "sit-ins" at whites-only lunch counters to protest those businesses' refusal to serve African Americans. The movement began with a group of four African-American students in Greensboro, North Carolina, and quickly spread to cities in New York, Virginia, Florida, Tennessee and other states. Following King's teachings of nonviolence, the students would sit at the lunch counters and refuse to leave until they were served. They were often spat upon, called names, and even beaten and arrested. But as soon as some were dragged off their seats, more stepped forward to take their place.

Baker was impressed with the youths' determination, especially since they started the sit-ins on their own. But she also realized the sit-ins lacked leadership, so she asked SCLC to sponsor a meeting of participating students at Shaw University on Easter weekend, 1960. More than 200 students attended.[6]

SCLC had expected the students to become part of its organization, but the students wanted to form their own group. Baker supported them. She had become tired of SCLC's leadership and what she viewed as a slow response to action, just as she had with the NAACP fourteen years earlier.[7] She viewed the youth as the torchbearers for the civil rights movement, so she resigned from SCLC and helped form the Student Nonviolent Coordinating Committee (SNCC) in October 1960. Serving as an adult adviser and role model for the group, Baker helped SNCC ignite the first student-activist civil rights movement in American history.[8]

The sit-ins cost businesses money. African Americans refused to patronize segregated lunch counters and whites stayed away because they were afraid of the often violent results. By the end of 1960, lunch counters across the country were beginning to integrate. Building on these victories, SNCC focused on other businesses that separated blacks and whites, slowly tearing down the walls of segregation.

"The [African-American] and white students, North and South, are seeking to rid America of the scourge of racial segregation and discrimination— not only at the lunch counters, but in every aspect of life," Baker wrote a few months after forming SNCC.[9]

When it came time to nominate a Democratic candidate for U.S. president in 1964, SNCC helped launch the Mississippi Freedom Democratic Party (MFDP). This was a political party that challenged the all-white Democratic party of Mississippi. The MFDP argued that the all-white party did not represent all the citizens of Mississippi and therefore should not be allowed to help nominate a candidate for president.

Baker headed the MFDP's offices and attended the convention in Atlantic City, New Jersey, to help the MFDP delegates take the place of the traditional Mississippi Democrats. The move was unsuccessful, but it laid the groundwork for the next presidential Democratic convention in 1968, where African Americans as well as whites represented Mississippi.

Through the late 1960s and early 1970s, Baker continued her work with SNCC. Now the organization branched out to protest the Vietnam War and formed the Poor People's Corporation to provide loans to self-help organizations. Throughout the 1970s, she traveled around the country raising

Fannie Lou Hamer (left) and Ella Baker at the 1964 Democratic National Party Convention.

awareness for social issues like women's rights and prison reform. In 1983, public television aired a documentary based on her life, *Fundi: The Story of Ella Baker. Fundi* is Swahili for "one who hands down a craft from one generation to the next."[10]

Baker died after years of poor health on her eighty-third birthday in 1986, and was buried in New York City. In 1994, she was inducted into the National Women's Hall of Fame in Seneca Falls, New York.

Ella Baker understood the importance of becoming involved in something if you wanted it to change. It was her life's philosophy. "[During the 1960s] you had to break through things to get what you wanted," she said shortly before her death. "You didn't just sit up there and think about it; it had to happen."[11]

3

Thurgood Marshall
(1908–1993)

In December 1952, Thurgood Marshall, an attorney for the National Association for the Advancement of Colored People (NAACP), argued before the Supreme Court that the separation of races was unconstitutional and therefore illegal. The only reason to continue the practice would be to make sure that "the people who were formerly in slavery, regardless of anything else, shall be kept as near that stage as possible," he said.[1]

The Supreme Court agreed, and in 1954 outlawed racial segregation in all schools. The fact that African Americans can now eat at the same restaurants, drink from the same water fountains and attend the same schools as whites might not have been possible without Marshall.

Thoroughgood Marshall was born July 2, 1908, in Baltimore, Maryland, the son of William Marshall, a waiter, and Norma Arica Marshall, a teacher. He was named after his paternal grandfather. In the second grade, he shortened his name to Thurgood because he was tired of spelling it out.[2]

Thurgood often got into trouble in school. As punishment, the principal would make him memorize a passage from the United States Constitution. The principal did not know it, but the punishment prepared Marshall for a lifetime of interpreting and defending the document. "Before I left that school, I knew the whole thing by heart," he remembered.[3]

But young Thurgood was troubled by the Thirteenth, Fourteenth, and Fifteenth Amendments of the Constitution. Enacted after the Civil War, the amendments abolished slavery, extended to blacks the same rights given to whites, and guaranteed them the right to vote. Marshall asked his father why, with such laws in place, whites seemed to have more rights than blacks. His father replied that the Constitution was a blueprint for the way things should be, not a description of the way they were. With those words, he set Marshall on the path to becoming a lawyer.[4]

When he graduated high school at age sixteen in 1925, Marshall went to college at Lincoln University, a black college in Chester, Pennsylvania. One day, he and his friends sat in the whites-only section of a movie theater in the nearby town of Oxford and refused to move. It was the first of many civil rights fights for Marshall.

Marshall was still in college in September 1929 when he married Vivian "Buster" Burey, a student at the University of Pennsylvania. He graduated from Lincoln University in 1930 and applied to the University of Maryland's law school, but was rejected. At the time, the University of Maryland did not admit black students. Marshall went to law school at Howard University in Washington, D.C., but the anger from being rejected by the University of Maryland would stay with him for years.

In 1925 many movie theaters throughout the country were segregated. African-American moviegoers were forced to use a separate entrance, as shown here.

In the early 1930s, there were few African-American lawyers in the United States. Marshall was determined not only to receive his law degree, but to become the best lawyer he could. With the guidance of Charles Houston, a professor at Howard, he discovered a passion for civil rights. Marshall watched Houston and other NAACP lawyers in the university's law library as they prepared their cases attacking segregation.

Marshall graduated first in his class from Howard in 1933, and opened his own practice in Baltimore. In 1934, he was hired by the Baltimore *Afro-American* newspaper to handle legal work. The newspaper's owners soon asked him to work for the local NAACP chapter. One of his first cases as a civil rights lawyer was an act of "sweet revenge": He brought suit against the University of Maryland and forced it to start admitting black students.[5]

After winning the University of Maryland case, Marshall toured the South with Houston, seeking cases they could represent to attack segregation. He eventually replaced Houston as the NAACP's chief counsel in 1938 and quit his law practice to work for the organization full-time. Throughout the 1940s, he continued to help people whose civil rights had been violated. When African Americans were drafted into the Korean War in the early 1950s, Marshall investigated charges that they were being mistreated by their white officers. He helped twenty black servicemen convicted of cowardice get their sentences reduced. In all, he won twenty-nine cases before the Supreme Court and lost only three. But, he would be best remembered for the 1954 case that ended segregation in schools.

The case, *Brown* v. *Board of Education of Topeka* (Kansas), was a class-action suit brought by African-American parents against school boards that required racial segregation in their schools. A class-action lawsuit is one filed by a person or group of persons on behalf of a large group with a common interest. At the time, white schools got much more taxpayer money than black schools. While the white schools were often nice brick buildings with modern textbooks, African-American schools were usually rundown wooden buildings with old textbooks.

The NAACP, with Marshall as chief council, took the case to the Supreme Court in 1952. They argued that segregation of schools violated the Fourteenth Amendment because it denied blacks the same opportunities as whites. The Supreme Court was divided on the issue. The court ordered both sides to come back the following session and answer five questions. Two questions asked about the intentions of the Fourteenth Amendment's framers—what did Congress have in mind when they wrote and then passed the amendment in 1868. Another asked about judicial power to order desegregation if those intentions were unclear. And two asked whether a court could order gradual desegregation and, if so, what form that desegregation should take.[6]

In the meantime, the chief justice of the Supreme Court, Fred Vinson, died. He was replaced by Earl Warren. Although no one knew how Warren would vote, he proved to be a strong supporter of desegregation. Warren wanted a unanimous ruling, because he felt a divided opinion would give white southerners an excuse to oppose the decision.[7] The court heard the case again in December 1953, and Warren urged the dissenting justices to change their minds.

On May 17, 1954, a unanimous decision was issued. The Supreme Court ruled that having separate schools for white and black children violated the Constitution. "To separate [black children] from others of similar age and qualifications solely because of their race generates a feeling of inferiority as to their status in the community that may affect their hearts and minds in a way unlikely ever to be undone," the court ruled. "In the field of public education the doctrine of 'separate but equal' has no place."[8]

It was the biggest civil rights victory since the years following the Civil War, but many southern schools still refused to let blacks enter. Many African-American students who tried to attend white schools were threatened. Marshall spent several more years helping them in the courts. For Marshall there was no room for compromise. "On the racial issue, you can't be a little bit wrong any more than you can be a little bit pregnant or a little bit dead," he said.[9]

In 1955, soon after the *Brown* decision, Marshall's wife, Vivian, died of cancer. Eleven months later, Marshall married Cecilia "Cissy" Suyat, a secretary for the NAACP. They had two sons, Thurgood Jr. and John. worse

In 1961, Marshall was appointed to the Second Court of Appeals by President John F. Kennedy. His appointment was approved by the United States Senate in 1962. Three years later, in 1965, he was appointed solicitor general by President Lyndon Johnson. It was considered a steppingstone to the Supreme Court, and in June 1967, Johnson nominated Marshall to be the first African American on the court. His appointment was confirmed by the Senate on August 30, 1967.

During Marshall's twenty-four years on the Supreme Court, he helped render decisions on many important cases. In 1971, the court upheld the right of newspapers to publish the Pentagon Papers, top-secret documents about America's involvement in Vietnam. In 1972, it ruled that the death penalty was unconstitutional. (The Supreme Court reversed this decision in 1976). In 1973, it upheld a woman's right to have an abortion in *Roe* v. *Wade*, a very controversial decision that is still being debated today. Marshall was a major figure in each of these decisions.

By the 1980s, there were new justices on the Supreme Court who were more conservative than their predecessors. Marshall was growing increasingly

Thurgood Marshall (left) consults with President Lyndon Johnson before being appointed Supreme Court justice.

frustrated with this more conservative stance, which he viewed as a threat to all the civil rights accomplishments made during the 1950s and 1960s.[10] More and more often, he was rendering dissents—legal disagreements—to the majority's rulings. But he refused to retire from what he viewed as his duty to those who needed him the most: minorities and the poor.

On June 27, 1991, Marshall announced he was retiring because of poor health. Less than two years later, on January 21, 1993, he died of heart failure at

Bethesda Naval Medical Center in Maryland. Thousands of people came to pay their last respects. Across the country, people mourned the loss of one of America's greatest civil rights leaders. Explaining Marshall's influence, Jesse Jackson remembered, "For most of us who grew up under segregation, we have never known a day without Thurgood Marshall hovering over us to protect us."[11]

4

Rosa Parks
(1913–   )

Rosa Parks was tired.

Not physically tired, even though she had worked all day and was eager to get home. She was mentally tired. She was sitting in her seat in the black section of the bus, just as the laws in Montgomery, Alabama, said African Americans should. When a group of white passengers got on the bus and found no empty seats in the white section, the driver demanded that Parks and three other African Americans give up their seats.

The other three blacks got up. Parks refused. The bus driver called the police, and five minutes later, she was arrested and taken to jail. With that simple act of defiance, Rosa Parks would kick-start the civil rights movement and begin a chain of events that would lead to desegregation in America.

"I did not feel any fear at sitting in the seat I was sitting in," Parks said years later. "All I felt was tired. Tired of seeing the bad treatment and disrespect of children, women, and men just because of the color of their skin. . . . Tired of being oppressed. I was just plain tired."[1]

Rosa Parks was born Rosa Louise McCauley on February 4, 1913, in Tuskegee, Alabama. She was the first child of James and Leona McCauley. Her father, a carpenter, left the family soon after Rosa's younger brother was born. With her children in tow, Leona, a teacher, moved in with her parents on a small farm in Pine Level, Alabama.

Rosa learned to be proud of who she was, even in the face of racism that denied African Americans the right to vote, eat, or go to school with whites. Her grandfather had been a slave who was treated badly by his master, and he vowed never to take abuse from anybody again. When the Ku Klux Klan terrorized black residents of Pine Level in the 1920s, Rosa stayed up with her grandfather as he waited with a shotgun for them to attack his home.

The attack never came, but Rosa never forgot the experience. "My grandfather was the one who instilled in my mother and her sisters, and in their children, that you don't put up with bad treatment from anybody," she said years later. "It was passed down almost in our genes."[2]

Parks attended school until the eleventh grade, when she had to drop out to care for her dying grandmother. In 1931, while she was in her late teens, she met Raymond Parks, a barber in downtown Montgomery. They were married on December 18, 1932. Raymond Parks was self-educated, and he encouraged Rosa to finish high school. She received her diploma in 1934.

Raymond Parks was a long-time member of the National Association for the Advancement of Colored People (NAACP). In the early 1930s, he helped the organization in its efforts to free the Scottsboro boys, nine young men falsely accused of raping a white woman in Scottsboro, Alabama. Rosa Parks also became active in the NAACP, becoming the secretary and later youth leader of its Montgomery branch.

Parks refused to be treated as inferior. Because of that attitude, she was thrown off a Montgomery city bus for the first time in 1943. African Americans had to pay at the front of the bus, then get off and enter through the back. Sometimes the bus driver would leave without them after they had paid. In 1943 Parks refused to get off the bus and go to the back. She was thrown off the bus by the same driver who tried to make her give up her seat twelve years later.

In 1954, the United States Supreme Court ruled that segregation in schools was unconstitutional. African Americans rejoiced. Many, including Parks,

Rosa Parks

thought the same idea should also be applied to public transportation.

"I don't think any segregation law angered black people in Montgomery more than bus segregation," Parks said. "More of us rode the buses than [whites] did, because more whites could afford cars. It was very humiliating, having to suffer the indignity of riding segregated buses twice a day, five days a week, to go downtown and work for white people."[3]

When Parks refused to leave her seat on December 1, 1955, she was not trying to start a movement. She never thought that her actions would ignite a spark that would eventually help topple segregation throughout the nation. She was just standing up for her rights. "I did not get on the bus to get arrested," she said later. "I got on the bus to go home."[4]

The NAACP had been looking for someone to be a plaintiff in a lawsuit against the city to end segregated busing, and Parks agreed to be that plaintiff. E. D. Nixon, president of the Montgomery NAACP, arranged a meeting with eighteen local ministers to mobilize community support. The ministers formed the Montgomery Improvement Association (MIA) and called on African Americans to boycott by refusing to ride the buses. Martin Luther King, Jr., pastor of the Dexter Avenue Baptist Church, was chosen to lead MIA.

Throughout the city, African Americans refused to ride buses. The MIA arranged car pools and bought station wagons to help blacks get to work. Black cab drivers dropped their usual forty-five-cent fares to ten cents, the same price as bus fare. Those who had no transportation simply walked. Without African-American riders, the buses lost money and eventually stopped running altogether.

City leaders tried everything in their power to stop the boycott and force blacks to ride the buses. Policemen arrested cab drivers who offered low fares. People waiting for car pools were harassed. King's and Nixon's homes were bombed. In February 1956, Parks, King and others were indicted by a grand jury on charges of illegal boycotting.

But the African Americans refused to budge. Like Parks, they were tired. A *Time* magazine article reported an incident in which an African-American minister, working for the car pool, stopped to pick up an elderly woman who had been walking. "Sister," he said, "aren't you getting tired?" The elderly woman replied, "My soul has been tired for a long time. Now my feet are tired, and my soul is resting."[5]

Finally, MIA's lawsuit made it all the way to the Supreme Court. On November 13, 1956, the Supreme Court ruled that segregation on buses was unconstitutional. The written order appeared on December 20, 1956, and the boycott was called off the next day. It had lasted 381 days.

The bus boycott received national media attention. Parks suddenly found herself in the spotlight. She was invited to many speaking engagements to

Rosa Parks being fingerprinted in Montgomery, Alabama. The photograph was taken the day Parks was indicted for illegal boycotting.

talk about her experiences. She accepted, even though she was uncomfortable with the attention.

In Montgomery, Parks was shunned by whites. She lost her job as a seamstress because of the boycott, and feared for her safety. Finally, in 1957, Parks and her family moved to Detroit.

Parks continued to be active in the NAACP and the civil rights movement during the 1960s. She attended the March on Washington in 1963 and joined in the final leg of King's civil rights march from Selma, Alabama, to Montgomery in 1965. In 1965, she also began work as a receptionist and office assistant for Congressman John Conyers in Detroit, and she held that job until her retirement in 1988.

Raymond Parks died of cancer in 1977. In tribute to him, Rosa Parks co-founded the Rosa and Raymond Parks Institute for Self-Development in 1987 to help youths realize their highest potential. The institute offers scholarships, courses in communication and economic skills, and political awareness.[6]

Today, Rosa Parks is considered the mother of the civil rights movement. She has received many honors. A bust of her was unveiled at the Smithsonian Institution in Washington, D.C., in 1991. She received an honorary degree from Japan's Soka University in 1994.

In 1999, Congress awarded Parks its highest honor: the Congressional Gold Medal. In voting to give her the award, members of Congress praised Parks for her defiant act that changed America. Representative John Lewis of Georgia, a veteran of the battle for civil rights explained, "Rosa Parks has taught me and an entire generation the power that one individual can have in standing up for what is right and for what is just."[7]

Still, there is one other honor that Parks appreciates. The bus that Parks was riding when she was arrested in 1955 was known as the Cleveland Avenue line. Today, Cleveland Avenue is called Rosa Parks Boulevard.[8]

5

Fannie Lou Hamer
(1917–1977)

Fannie Lou Hamer is not well known as a civil rights leader. She was not the head of a national organization like Martin Luther King, Jr., and she was not a lawyer like Thurgood Marshall. She lived and died poor in the same community in which she had picked cotton most of her life. Yet many of the reforms she helped bring about are still felt throughout the United States to this day.

Hamer was born Fannie Lou Townsend on October 6, 1917, in Montgomery County, Mississippi. She was the twentieth child of Jim and Ella Townsend. Her parents were sharecroppers, farmers who lived on the land they farmed and had to share their profits with the landowners. All too often, white landowners took most of the profit from the sharecroppers' labor, while the sharecroppers, many of whom were African American, kept very little of the money and lived in poverty.

Hamer's family was no exception. They were so poor that often all they had to eat were vegetables and flour gravy. One year, Jim Townsend finally scrounged up enough money to rent some land, three mules, two cows and farm tools. The family finally had some hope of escaping their severe poverty. But that all ended when a white man poisoned their animals.

"He couldn't stand to see [African Americans] doing all right," Hamer said years later. "We went right back to the bottom again, and that's where we stayed—right back sharecropping."[1]

When Fannie Lou was two, her family moved to Sunflower County, Mississippi. Fannie Lou began picking cotton at age six and left school after the sixth grade to work in the fields full time. Her mother was a great influence on her and taught her to never be ashamed of her skin color. "God made you black. Respect yourself," her mother told her.[2]

In 1944, Fannie Lou married Perry "Pap" Hamer, a tractor driver. They later adopted two daughters, Dorothy Jean and Vergie. For the next eighteen years, the Hamers continued to sharecrop. It seemed they were destined to live the rest of their days in obscurity, slaving over the land and scraping out a meager existence.

Still, Hamer never stopped dreaming of a better life. "Sometimes I be working in the fields and I get so tired I'd say to the people picking cotton with me, 'Hard as we have to work for nothing, there *must* be some way we can change this," she told a magazine reporter in the 1960s.[3]

In the summer of 1962, that chance came. Some civil rights workers came to speak at a church in Ruleville, Mississippi, not far from where the Hamers lived. It was the first time Hamer had heard freedom songs and the demand that African Americans be given equal rights. When the call came for a show of hands of those who wanted to register to vote, Hamer's was one of the first up.

Even though the Fifteenth and Nineteenth Amendments guaranteed the right for everyone to vote, many southern states found ways to exclude African Americans. One way they did this was to require that voters pay a tax just to vote. Few poor African Americans could afford this "poll tax." In other states, like Mississippi, state officials required people to pass complicated tests before they could register to vote. Often, they only asked black voters to pass these tests. Hamer's first attempt to register, on August 31, 1962, failed because the white men registering voters demanded that she pass such a test.

When Hamer went home, the owner of the land Hamer lived on and farmed tried to get her to go back and take her name off the register. She refused. "I didn't go down there to register for you," Hamer

Fannie Lou Hamer

told him. "I went down to register for myself." The landowner evicted Hamer from her home.[4]

Hamer left her family and stayed with friends in Ruleville. Even in Ruleville she faced violence and intimidation, but that just made Hamer more determined to fight. She returned to her family, and in the fall of 1962, she accepted an invitation from the Student Nonviolent Coordinating Committee (SNCC) to train for civil rights work in Nashville, Tennessee. In December 1962, she registered to vote again. This time, she was successful.

Hamer's speaking manner and beautiful singing voice helped make her a key figure in the civil rights movement. People often gathered at her home to listen to her speak and sing. One of her favorites was a gospel song, "This Little Light of Mine." "All my life I've been sick and tired," she told a magazine reporter. "Now I'm tired of being sick and tired."[5]

Hamer's work placed her in constant physical danger. In 1963, Hamer and other civil rights workers were arrested in Winona, Mississippi. At the Winona jail, she was beaten severely by two African Americans at the command of white police officers. Fortunately, other civil rights workers, including Andrew Young of the Southern Christian Leadership Conference, learned of the arrests and rushed to the civil rights workers' aid.

The Winona jail attack caused injuries that affected Hamer for the rest of her life. But it did not lessen her resolve. In 1964, she ran for Congress, something that was unheard of at the time for an African-American woman. Hamer did not win, but she remained active in Mississippi politics.

In the summer of 1964, SNCC launched a campaign in Mississippi called Freedom Summer. Members of the organization, including Hamer, held voter registration drives, established "freedom schools" for African-American children, and opened community centers where poor African Americans could obtain legal and medical assistance.

SNCC also established the Mississippi Freedom Democratic Party (MFDP), a new political party. By August 1964, more than 80,000 African Americans had joined MFDP, and they took their challenge to the Democratic National Convention in Atlantic City, New Jersey.[6]

The purpose of a national convention is to have delegates from every state choose a presidential nominee for the party. MFDP demanded that four of its members, including Hamer, be seated as Mississippi's delegates, because the all-white Mississippi Democratic Party would not let African Americans join. On the first day of the convention, Hamer was the star witness in MFDP's case before the national Democratic Party's Credentials Committee. Her testimony was televised to the entire nation. She spoke of her savage beating in jail and demanded that African Americans be given their constitutional rights. "If the Freedom

Fannie Lou Hamer testifying before the Credentials Committee of the 1964 Democratic National Convention.

Democratic Party is not seated now, I question America," she said.[7]

President Lyndon Johnson offered MFDP a compromise that would allow two of its delegates to be seated along with the white Mississippi delegates, but they would be "at large" members who would not officially represent Mississippi. The MFDP refused. Talking to television reporters later, Hamer called the compromise "token rights, on the back row, the same we got in Mississippi. We didn't come all this way for that mess again."[8]

Despite its failure to seat delegates in 1964, the MFDP's actions paved the way for success at the next convention in 1968. At that convention, held in Chicago, Hamer was among several African Americans seated as delegates to the national Democratic Party.

Hamer's television appearances at the conventions gained her national recognition. But she shunned the spotlight and instead chose to fight inequality and poverty from her own home in Ruleville, Mississippi.

In 1968, Hamer created Pig Bank with the help of the National Council of Negro Women to help raise food for the poor. In 1969, she formed the Freedom Farm Cooperative to help needy families raise food and livestock. Anyone could participate in the food programs. "The cry of hunger is the cry of hunger whether it comes from black, brown or red," she said.[9]

Hamer ran for office again in 1971, this time for the Mississippi state senate. Once again, she lost. She wanted to run for governor, but her health was deteriorating due to cancer and the injuries she suffered at the Winona jail. She died at age 60 on March 14, 1977.

Thousands of people came to Fannie Lou Hamer's funeral, and at the end of the service, everyone sang "This Little Light of Mine." She was buried in Ruleville, where her tombstone reads, "I am sick and tired of being sick and tired."[10]

6

Malcolm X
(1925–1965)

During his lifetime, no civil rights leader was more controversial than Malcolm X. When others were preaching nonviolence to achieve African-American rights, Malcolm X preached that blacks should do whatever was necessary to obtain those rights, even if it meant using violence.[1]

But no matter what view one takes of Malcolm X, his impact on the civil rights movement cannot be denied. He taught African Americans to stand up for themselves and be proud of their race; he was one of the first to call himself "Afro-American."[2] His cultural influence is viewed by many to be second only to that of Martin Luther King, Jr. "He made [young African Americans] proud of themselves and proud of being black," said Andrew Young, another leader in the civil rights movement.[3]

Malcolm X was born Malcolm Little on May 19, 1925 in Omaha, Nebraska, one of six children born to Earl and Louise Little. His mother's father, whom she never met, was white, and it was from him that Malcolm inherited a fair complexion and red hair. Afterwards he was ashamed of those traits.[4]

Earl Little, a Baptist minister, preached the teachings of Marcus Garvey, a black leader of the 1920s who started the "Back-to-Africa" movement. When Malcolm was six, the family moved to Lansing, Michigan, because they had received death threats. Angered by Earl Little's teachings, white supremacists burned down the family's house in 1929. In 1931, Malcolm's father was run over by a streetcar. His family suspected he had been murdered.

Earl Little's death left his family in poverty. He had taken out two life insurance policies, but one of the insurance companies said his death was a suicide and refused to pay. Destitute, the family often ate dandelion greens to survive. Malcolm began to steal food. He was caught and sent to a foster home and eventually a detention home.

Malcolm attended Mason Junior High School while under foster care. He did well in school until an incident in eighth-grade English class. The teacher asked the students what they wanted to be when they grew up. Malcolm said he wanted to be a lawyer. The teacher told Malcolm that was an unrealistic goal for an African American. "The more I thought afterwards about what he said, the more uneasy it made me," Malcolm said later. "It was then that I began to change—inside."[5]

Malcolm quit school after the eighth grade and moved to Boston to live with his half sister, Ella (Earl Little's daughter from a previous marriage). He fell in love with the Boston nightlife and danced, drank alcohol, and smoked marijuana. To make his hair straight, he started "conking" it by applying a form of lye. If left on too long, the lye could burn the scalp. At the time, he liked the look. But later, he would call it his "first really big step toward self-degradation." In his autobiography, Malcolm noted that many young African Americans at that time had been so "brainwashed into believing that black people are 'inferior'—and the white people 'superior' —that they will even violate or mutilate their God-created bodies to try to look 'pretty' by white standards."[6]

Malcolm settled in Harlem, a black community in New York, and began dealing drugs. After a dispute over a gambling debt nearly cost him his life, he moved back to Boston and set up a burglary ring. He was eventually caught and was sentenced to ten years in prison in February 1946.

While in prison, Malcolm was introduced to the Nation of Islam by his family. Accepting only African Americans as members, the Nation of Islam was headed by Elijah Muhammad, who preached that the only way black Americans could gain equality was to form their own nation. Malcolm was excited by this new group and began writing to Elijah Muhammad every day from prison. To make his letters sound more articulate, he became an avid reader and carefully studied every page of the dictionary to expand his vocabulary.

When he was released on parole in 1952, the twenty-seven-year-old Malcolm jumped headfirst into a new role as a member of the Nation of Islam. He had already stopped conking his hair and using drugs and alcohol as the religion dictated. Following the tradition of the Nation of Islam, Malcolm dropped "Little" as his last name and replaced it with "X." Family names of many African Americans came from their former slave owners, and Malcolm wanted to cut this bond to slavery. In 1958, he married Betty X, who was also a member of the Nation of Islam. They had six daughters.

Malcolm X quickly became chief spokesman for the Nation of Islam, whose members were called "Black Muslims" by the press. His fiery speeches made him the group's most visible minister. Other civil rights leaders were organizing peaceful marches to integrate schools, restaurants and other public places. Malcolm X did not think this was the way to achieve equal rights. African Americans were going to have to separate themselves from whites to have equality, and they were going to have to respond to violence with violence, he said: "It is criminal to

Malcolm X at a news conference.

teach a man not to defend himself when he is the constant victim of brutal attacks."[7]

The Nation of Islam appointed Malcolm X to be its first national minister in 1962. A year later, his remarks began a strain that led to his separation from the group. In November 1963, President John F. Kennedy was shot and killed in Dallas, Texas. When asked what he thought about the assassination, Malcolm X replied that it was a case of "the chickens coming home to roost."[8] The Nation of Islam suspended him from speaking in public for ninety days.

At first, Malcolm X agreed to the suspension. But he believed the real reason for the order was that Elijah Muhammad was jealous of Malcolm's attention in the press and angry because Malcolm X had questioned his morals.[9] In March 1964, he left the Nation of Islam and formed his own group, Muslim Mosque, Incorporated.

In April 1964, Malcolm X made a *hajj* (pilgrimage) to Mecca, a holy city in Saudi Arabia. Muslims try to make at least one trip to Mecca in their lifetime if they are physically able. Malcolm X saw white and black Muslims worshipping, eating, and dwelling together. For Malcolm X, who was used to segregation in America, it was an amazing sight.

"There were tens of thousands of pilgrims, from all over the world," he wrote in a letter to the American press. "They were of all colors, from blue-eyed blonds to black-skinned Africans. But we were all participating in the same ritual, displaying a spirit of unity and brotherhood that my experiences in America had led me to believe never could exist between the white and the non-white."[10] He signed the letter with a new name: El-Hajj Malik El-Shabazz.

When he returned from Mecca, Malcolm announced he was organizing a nonreligious group called the Organization of Afro-American Unity (OAAU). The purpose of OAAU, he said, was to push for more political and economic opportunities for African Americans. Malcolm X also announced that his trip to Mecca had changed his views on the separation of races. "A blanket indictment of all white people is as wrong as when whites make blanket indictments against blacks," he explained.[11]

Meanwhile, tensions with the Nation of Islam were still very high. Malcolm X's house was fire-bombed on Feb. 13, 1965, and he blamed the Black Muslims. The Nation of Islam was trying to kill him, he said, because he had spoken out publicly against Elijah Muhammad.[12]

One week later, on Feb. 21, 1965, Malcolm X was shot and killed by three African-American men while giving a speech during an OAAU rally at the Audubon Ballroom in New York. He was thirty-nine years old. While the Nation of Islam denied involvement in his death, the three men who shot him were allegedly connected with the Black Muslims. Malcolm X's followers retaliated by fire-bombing

Black Muslim mosques in Harlem and San Francisco.

Malcolm's popularity grew even more after his death. His autobiography, coauthored by Alex Haley, became a bestseller. Young African Americans began to chant "black power" in the late 1960s, seizing upon Malcolm X's message of self-reliance. In 1992, his story was made into a film, *Malcolm X*. Young people began wearing hats and T-shirts with a large "X" on them.

The beliefs and tactics of Malcolm X were different from most in the civil rights struggle of the

The interior of the Audubon Ballroom in New York City, where Malcolm X was assassinated.

1960s. He did not actively push for integration, he did not participate in marches, and he did not believe nonviolence was the only way to achieve change. What he did believe was that blacks should be proud of who they were and take it upon themselves to make their lives better.

"When historians, in the time to come, look back upon the civil rights struggles of the mid-20th century, there are two men whose lives they cannot possibly ignore—Martin Luther King, Jr., and Malcolm Little, better known throughout the world as Malcolm X," *Ebony* magazine stated shortly after his death. "They followed different paths that brought them both into the international limelight, espousing radically different philosophies and yet, strangely, working toward the same end—the winning of the dignity of manhood for the black man in America."[13]

7

Martin Luther King, Jr.
(1929–1968)

On August 28, 1963, more than 250,000 people gathered at the Lincoln Memorial in Washington, D.C. From all over the country they came by bus, train, car, even on foot for the March on Washington. Young and old, poor and wealthy, black and white all joined together for a common cause.

As dusk began to settle, the event's main speaker approached the podium before the Lincoln Memorial. All grew quiet as a thirty-three-year-old minister from Atlanta, Georgia, began speaking:

> I have a dream that my four little children will one day live in a nation where they will not be judged by the color of their skin but by the content of their character. . . . That one day. . . little black boys and black girls will be able to join

hands with little white boys and white girls as brothers and sisters.

And when we allow freedom to ring . . . we will be able to speed up that day when all of God's children . . . will be able to join hands and to sing in the words of the old Negro spiritual, 'Free at last, free at last; thank God Almighty, we are free at last!'[1]

With those words, Martin Luther King, Jr., would forever link himself and the civil rights movement into one image.

Born on January 15, 1929, in Atlanta, Martin Luther King, Jr., was one of three sons of a Baptist minister. He learned at a young age that blacks and whites were treated differently. As a high school junior, he traveled to southern Georgia with his speech teacher to compete in a debating contest. He won an award and was overjoyed until, on the bus ride home, he and his teacher were forced to give up their seats to white passengers and stand all the way to Atlanta. For young Martin, it was a life-changing experience. "It was a night I'll never forget," he said years later. "I don't think I have ever been so deeply angry in my life."[2]

King graduated from high school at age fifteen in 1944 and enrolled at Morehouse College in Atlanta. In 1947, he was ordained a minister and was made assistant pastor at his father's church while still in college. He received a bachelor's degree in sociology in 1948 and a ministerial degree at Crozier

Theological Seminary in Chester, Pennsylvania, in 1951. He married Coretta Scott, a girl he had met in college, in 1953. They had four children.

At first, King seemed to be on the path to a quiet life. He became minister of the Dexter Avenue Baptist Church in Montgomery, Alabama, in 1954, and obtained a doctorate degree in theology from Boston College the next year. But just as a bus ride in his youth had affected his outlook on life, another bus ride in Montgomery changed his life forever.

In December 1955, Rosa Parks, an African-American woman in Montgomery, refused to give her bus seat to a white person and was arrested. Local African Americans called for a boycott and formed the Montgomery Improvement Association (MIA) to end such racist policies. For their president, they elected King.

At the time, few people knew of King. Some had doubts about his leadership ability because he was only twenty-six. But when the young minister addressed the protesters, fears were laid to rest. "We, the disinherited of this land, we who have been oppressed so long, are tired of going through the long night of captivity," he said. "And now we are reaching out for the daybreak of freedom and justice and equality."[3]

Under King's leadership, MIA organized car pools and raised money so churches could buy station wagons and drive people to work. Those who did not have transportation walked. All over

Montgomery, empty buses roamed the streets because black people refused to ride. The boycott cost the bus company money. Finally, after more than a year, the United States Supreme Court ruled that segregation on buses was illegal. The MIA had won.

Throughout the boycott, King had advocated a policy of nonviolent protest. Mahatma Gandhi had used such protests to help India gain its independence from Great Britain during the 1940s. King had learned of Gandhi's teachings while a student at Crozier. Following the boycott, the Kings traveled to India to study Gandhi's teachings further.[4]

In 1957, King and other ministers formed the Southern Christian Leadership Conference (SCLC) to campaign for civil rights in the South. King continued to work with SCLC for the rest of his life. In 1958, King published a book on the bus boycott called *Stride Toward Freedom: The Montgomery Story.* During a book signing in September 1958, he narrowly escaped death when he was stabbed in the chest with a letter opener by a mentally ill woman.[5] King recovered and moved his family back to Atlanta in 1960 after being named co-pastor with his father at Ebenezer Baptist Church.

By the early 1960s, the civil rights movement was in full force. African-American college students held sit-ins at restaurants in the South by sitting at whites-only lunch counters and refusing to leave until they were served. Other students, both black and white, known as freedom riders, went on bus tours around the South to ensure that blacks were allowed equal access to restrooms, restaurants and other public places. Civil rights workers helped African Americans register to vote.

Civil rights activists did their work at great risk. Many of them were threatened, taunted, beaten, and even killed. Being jailed for protesting was almost commonplace. Despite these risks civil rights workers persevered.

King was no exception. His house was bombed. King received many death threats, but he did not give up. While he was held in a Birmingham jail in April 1963 for participating in a public demonstration,

Martin Luther King, Jr., at a news conference.

King wrote a letter to some white ministers who had criticized his actions. They thought the civil rights battle should be fought only in the courts. King's response, which became known as "Letter from Birmingham City Jail," was soon used as the philosophy for the civil rights movement. "For years now I have heard the words 'Wait!'" he wrote. "This 'Wait' has almost always meant 'Never'. . . . We have waited for more than 340 years for our constitutional and God-given rights."[6]

In July 1964, a new Civil Rights Act was passed. The act made it illegal to refuse to serve African Americans in public places or to deny anyone a job based on their race. Later that year, King was awarded the Nobel Peace Prize.[7]

On March 7, 1965, SCLC tried to lead a march from Selma, Alabama, to Montgomery to demand voting rights for blacks. The marchers were turned back at a bridge in Selma by police, who beat and tear-gassed them. The brutality was televised, and many whites, North and South, were upset by the police violence against the nonviolent marchers.[8] King led a second march from Selma to Montgomery two weeks later. The Selma demonstrations helped bring national attention to the cause, and on August 6, the Voting Rights Act of 1965 was signed into law.

After Selma, King expanded his causes. In 1965, he tried unsuccessfully to end discrimination in Chicago housing. In June 1966, he participated in a march to encourage black voting in Mississippi. In

1967, he spoke out against the Vietnam War and launched the Poor People's Campaign, an SCLC program designed to help poor people of all races. To King, it did not matter what color people were. All that mattered was that they needed help.

In April 1968, King went to Memphis, Tennessee, to help striking sanitation workers gain fair job benefits. During a speech to the strikers on April 3, he talked about threats on his life. "I don't know what will happen now. We've got some difficult days ahead. But it really doesn't matter now, because I've

The March on Selma, Alabama, pictured here, brought national attention to the civil rights cause.

been to the mountaintop. And I don't mind," King explained. "I'm not worried about anything. I'm not fearing any man. Mine eyes have seen the glory of the coming of the Lord!"[9]

On the next day, April 4, 1968, Martin Luther King, Jr., was shot and killed by James Earl Ray, a white man. King was only thirty-nine years old. Riots broke out across the country when people heard the news.

King's message and his legacy live on. Of all the people who gave to the civil rights cause, King is the one who instantly comes to mind when people talk about the struggle to obtain equal rights for African Americans during the 1950s and the 1960s. In many people's eyes, the civil rights movement would not have existed without him.

On Martin Luther King, Jr.'s tombstone is this inscription: "Free at last, free at last, thank God Almighty, I'm free at last."[10]

8

Andrew Young
(1932–   )

When Martin Luther King, Jr., was demonstrating for civil rights during the 1960s, he had a young minister named Andrew Young at his side to give advice and help make plans. When King was arrested in Birmingham, Alabama, during a march in 1963, Young negotiated with the city to avoid violence. When demonstrators were attacked by police in Selma, Alabama, in 1965, Young was there to aid the wounded. And when King was shot and killed in Memphis, Tennessee, in 1968, Young was one of those who rushed to his aid.

Andrew Jackson Young, Jr., was born March 12, 1932, in New Orleans, Louisiana. He was the son of Andrew Young, Sr., a dentist, and Daisy Fuller Young, a former schoolteacher. The elder of two boys, Young was raised with a strong religious faith. His parents taught him that any obstacles could be overcome with a firm belief in God, a good education, and hard work.

These lessons helped Young throughout his life. "Daddy taught me that racism was a sickness and to have compassion for racist whites as I would have compassion for a polio victim," he would recall years later. "Racism wasn't a problem with me, he told me, it was a problem they had."[1]

A bright student, Young skipped the first and second grades and entered Valena C. Jones Elementary School, a black public school, in the third grade. He attended the Gilbert Academy, a private school in New Orleans, from eighth to twelfth grades, and enrolled in his parent's alma mater, Dillard University, at age fifteen. He transferred to the prestigious Howard University in Washington, D.C., for his sophomore year of college.

Throughout his life, Young was expected by his parents to take over his father's dental practice. But when he graduated from Howard University with a bachelor's degree in biology in 1951, he did not know what he wanted to do.

As his parents drove him home after his graduation, they stopped at Lincoln Academy in Kings Mountain, North Carolina. Their church was holding a summer conference there. Young met John Heinrich, a young white minister who was on his way to the African nation of Rhodesia (now called

Zimbabwe) to serve as a missionary. Young was impressed with Heinrich's dedication and began to think about joining the ministry himself.

That thought was cemented soon afterwards, when he raced a group of other youths to the top of a mountain peak. When he reached the top, Young marveled at the beauty of the trees, the landscape and the vegetation that surrounded him. "Suddenly, at the top of Kings Mountain, my whole life began anew," he wrote in his 1994 memoir, *A Way Out of No Way*. "If everything else in the world was part of God's order, then I, too, must be a part of some plan of the Creator."[2]

Young finally told his parents of his decision to become a minister later that summer. His father was extremely disappointed because ministers did not make much money. He was concerned Young would not be able to support a family.[3] But Young was sure of his choice and entered Hartford Seminary in Hartford, Connecticut, in spring of 1952. That summer, he met Jean Childs, a college student who, like Young, was determined to end unjust racial laws in America. They were married on June 7, 1954, and had four children.

Shortly after getting married, Young received his first church assignment as a summer assistant at Bethany Congregational Church in Thomasville, Georgia. After graduating from Hartford and being ordained a minister in the United Church of Christ, he returned to Bethany and became its pastor in

Andrew Young

January 1955. He held his first voter registration drive for African Americans the following year.

In 1957, Young accepted a job with the National Council of Churches of Christ in New York as an associate director in its youth department and helped organize interracial conferences for youth throughout the South. In February 1960, Andrew and Jean saw televised news reports of four African-American students in Greensboro, North Carolina. The students had sat at a lunch counter reserved for whites and refused to move. It was the beginning of the sit-in movement that soon spread throughout the country. The Youngs knew immediately that they wanted to be part of the movement.

In 1961, Young moved his family to Atlanta, Georgia, and started a leadership training program. The program was administered by the United Church of Christ and affiliated with Martin Luther King, Jr.'s, Southern Christian Leadership Conference (SCLC). In the beginning, Young took a behind-the-scenes role by training African Americans for work in the civil rights movement. One of his recruits was Fannie Lou Hamer, [a sharecropper] from Ruleville, Mississippi. Hamer would soon become a major player in the movement.

When SCLC decided to hold a major demonstration in Birmingham, Alabama, in 1963, Young was selected to negotiate with the city's leaders. SCLC wanted an end to segregation in Birmingham in the hopes that it would kick-start similar efforts in other cities and result in a national civil rights bill. "We made it clear that the fear of jail or even death could no longer keep us locked into a system that required us to accept a false inferiority, and in which white citizens enjoyed a superiority based solely on race," Young later wrote.[4]

The Birmingham demonstrations lasted for weeks. Hundreds of participants, including King, were beaten, jailed, or both. The protests, coupled with a boycott of businesses in the city, finally caused Birmingham officials to agree to end unjust racial practices. It was the first major victory for SCLC, and it helped pave the way for the passage of a civil rights bill in 1964.

Young was selected as SCLC's executive director in spring 1964 and became one of King's closest advisers. Riding on the success of Birmingham, SCLC launched similar campaigns in St. Augustine, Florida, in 1964, and in Selma, Alabama, in 1965. Like Birmingham, these demonstrations resulted in police brutality and arrests. But also like Birmingham, the nonviolent campaigns helped break down the walls of segregation.

By 1967, SCLC had decided to expand its efforts to include not just African Americans, but poor people of all races. The Poor People's Campaign was spearheaded by King to press for reforms that would help bring people out of poverty. King would not live to see this campaign come to pass. On April 4, 1968, he was shot and killed outside his hotel room in

In Birmingham, Alabama, police used firehoses against nonviolent civil rights protesters.

Memphis, Tennessee. Young was in the parking lot of the hotel when it happened. Like millions of people throughout the world, Young was heartbroken over King's death.

The Poor People's Campaign went on as planned in 1968, but it would be one of the last major campaigns of SCLC. In 1970, Young decided he could best serve the civil rights movement as a member of Congress. "Instead of marching around the Capitol and trying to influence things, I thought I should walk into the Capitol and get some legislation enacted," he said.[5]

Young received the Democratic nomination for a seat in Atlanta's Fifth Congressional District but lost in 1970. He ran again in 1972 and won, becoming the first black congressman from the Deep South since 1901. Young was reelected to Congress twice.[6]

In 1977, President Jimmy Carter asked Young to be the United States Ambassador to the United Nations. He soon established a reputation as an independent and influential ambassador while pushing for human rights reforms throughout the world. However, in 1979, he caused an uproar when he met with a representative of the Palestine Liberation Organization, which at that time sponsored terrorism in the Middle East. Young resigned soon afterward.[7]

But it was not Andrew Young's style to quit. In 1982, he became the mayor of Atlanta and was reelected in 1985. He played a major role in bringing the Olympics to Atlanta in 1996 and was co-chairman of the Atlanta Committee for the Olympic Games. His wife, Jean, died of cancer in September 1994. He married Carolyn McClain, a fifth-grade teacher, in 1996.[8]

Today, Young is a sought-after speaker and a respected leader in the civil rights arena that he has helped shape for more than forty years. In many ways, the spirit of Martin Luther King still lives inside him. "[King] left his mark on me, both in indelible memories and in the spiritual and practical lessons of our trials and triumphs," Young said in 1996. "It is by the quality of those days that I have come to measure my own continuing journey."[9]

9

Julian Bond
(1940–   )

In 1954, Julian Bond was a young teenager when the United States Supreme Court handed down the landmark decision in *Brown* v. *Board of Education of Topeka* (Kansas), that ended the separation of races in the schools. At the time, he did not think much about it—as far as he was concerned, he was going to follow in his father's footsteps as president of Lincoln University in Pennsylvania. As an African-American child, he thought any political goals other than that were unrealistic.[1]

That all changed on March 15, 1960, when he participated in his first sit-in at a whites-only lunch counter. With that act, he realized that the spark that had been ignited with *Brown* could be fanned into a flame and bring to African Americans what had been unthinkable since the Civil War: equality. "On that day, I joined hands with millions of other Americans in different cities, in different states, who took risks during those years to create the civil rights movement," he wrote more than twenty-five years later.[2]

Few people in the civil rights movement took more risks or gained more influence than Julian Bond. Over the course of three decades, he has been a state representative, a senator, a television host, a respected scholar and speaker, and most recently chairman of the National Association for the Advancement of Colored People (NAACP). By

Throughout the South, African Americans could not eat at lunch counters, like this one, until after a wave of sit-in protests.

thrusting himself into the civil rights movement, he made a better life for himself and in the process helped pave the way for millions of others.

Horace Julian Bond was born January 14, 1940, the second of three children. His parents, Horace Mann Bond and Julia Washington Bond, lived in rural Georgia. Because none of the good hospitals in Georgia would accept African-American patients, they went to Nashville, Tennessee, for Julian's birth. Horace Bond was instrumental in the brewing civil rights movement during the 1950s, preparing a legal brief for the *Brown* case.

To young Julian, the civil rights movement was just an abstract idea. He was more interested in his job running a coffee shop or in writing poetry than in changing society.[3] However, because he came from six generations of college graduates, he decided to follow the family tradition and attend Morehouse College in Atlanta, Georgia. It was a decision that would change his life.

On February 1, 1960, a group of college students in Greensboro, North Carolina, decided to challenge segregation at an whites-only lunch counter at a Woolworth's department store by sitting at the counter and refusing to move. The event became known as the first "sit-in," and the practice soon spread to other college campuses. One of Bond's friends showed him a newspaper article on the Greensboro sit-in and suggested they do the same in Atlanta. The two formed a small group, the

Committee on Appeal for Human Rights, and held their first sit-in at the Atlanta City Hall cafeteria on March 15, 1960.

As the sit-ins began to spread throughout the country, the Southern Christian Leadership Conference (SCLC), led by Martin Luther King, Jr., invited Bond and other participating students to a conference at Shaw University in North Carolina. The aim of SCLC was to absorb the sit-in groups. But the students thought SCLC's methods of fighting segregation through peaceful marches and court cases were too slow. "The institution and its politics just seemed so out of touch to us," Bond said years later. "They opposed the sit-ins. They didn't like direct action. They didn't like civil disobedience. They believed in law and litigation. And we were tired of that. We didn't want that. It took too long."[4]

Instead of joining SCLC, the students formed their own group, the Student Nonviolent Coordinating Committee (SNCC). Bond became SNCC's communications director and traveled throughout the South with other students to spread the group's message. In 1961, he dropped out of college to marry Alice Clopton, a student at Atlanta's Spelman College. By 1964, the couple had two children with a third on the way, and the strain began to bear down on him.[5] Bond began to worry about providing for his family. So when a group of SNCC members approached him with the idea of running as a candidate in the Georgia Democratic primary, he agreed and left his job as communications director in September 1965.

In 1965, Congress passed the Voter's Rights Act, which ended almost 100 years of Jim Crow laws that prevented African Americans from voting. As a result, many more blacks voted in 1965 than had in any previous year.[6] Bond, who was only twenty-six, was one of the political candidates who benefited. He won 84 percent of the vote in the race for a seat in the Georgia House of Representatives.[7] But what began as a great victory soon turned sour.

Four days before the new legislative session began in January 1966, SNCC issued a statement protesting the Vietnam War. When asked how he felt, Bond said he admired those who protested the war. "I admire people who take an action, and I admire people who feel strongly enough about their convictions to take an action like that knowing the consequences they will face," he said.[8] The Georgia legislature called Bond's remarks "treasonous" and refused to let him take his seat as a member of the House of Representatives.[9]

The legislature's action immediately sparked protests. Twenty-three United States congressmen sent a telegram to the Georgia governor protesting the action. Martin Luther King, Jr., led a 1,000-person march on the capitol in Atlanta. Two more elections were held, with Bond emerging the victor both times, but the legislature still refused to seat him. Finally, in December 1966, the Supreme Court ruled that the Georgia legislature had denied Bond freedom of speech and must seat him. Bond was finally allowed to take office the following January.

Bond's fight had made national news, and by 1967, he was a well-known figure. In 1968, he became the first African American nominated to be vice president. He had to withdraw from the race because he was only twenty-eight and did not meet the age requirement for the job. Still, many began to view Bond as a symbol of the new wave of African-American politicians.[10]

Bond spent all of the 1970s and most of the 1980s working in the Georgia legislature, first as a member of the House of Representatives and then, beginning in 1975, as a member of the state Senate. He also was much in demand as a speaker on civil rights issues and helped campaign for other African-American candidates running for political office.

In 1986, Bond gave up his Senate seat to run for United States House of Representatives against his long-time friend and SNCC colleague John Lewis. The campaign turned ugly, with Lewis accusing Bond of drug use. Bond lost the election. In 1989, Bond and his wife divorced after twenty-eight years of marriage. They had five children.[11]

Not all was bad for Bond during this period. He continued to be in demand as a public speaker. He hosted a television program, *America's Black Forum*. He narrated *Eyes on the Prize*, a documentary on the civil rights movement. He began teaching at the

Julian Bond in the Georgia House of Representatives.

University of Virginia and American University. His personal life also began to look up again when he married Pamela Sue Horowitz, a Washington, D.C., attorney, on March 17, 1990.

In 1998, Bond was named chairman of the board of the National Association for the Advancement of Colored People. Bond had been a member since high school. Now fifty-eight years old, he was ready for the task at hand. A reporter for *Time* magazine asked Bond about what issues the NAACP would be dealing with in the year 2000 and beyond. "It's still white supremacy," he explained. "It ensures them positions in employment and college admissions they otherwise might not have. It still puts a lid on the dreams of black people."[12]

Julian Bond, the young man who had entered the civil rights arena as a college student by sitting at a segregated lunch counter, is still fighting for equal rights more than thirty-five years later. But, as he acknowledges, the fight may be a little bit easier today thanks to the sacrifices he and so many others made those many years ago.

Jesse Jackson
(1941–   )

The Reverend Jesse Jackson has been called many things throughout his almost forty-year involvement in the civil rights movement: activist, politician, egomaniac, nationalist, even the heir to Martin Luther King, Jr. He refers to himself simply as a "country preacher" who does the will of God.[1] But both admirers and critics alike agree he has been an important leader in the struggle for civil rights.

Jesse Jackson was born Jesse L. Burns in Greenville, South Carolina, on October 8, 1941. His mother, Helen Burns, was an unwed teenager whose affair with a married man resulted in Jesse's birth. When he was three years old, Jesse's mother married Charles Jackson, a World War II veteran. They soon had a son, Charles Jackson, Jr.

Life in Greenville was hard for young Jesse. He grew up in poverty and was often teased by other children. When Charles, Jr., was born, Jesse was sent to live with his grandmother because the Jacksons could not afford to care for two children. He did not live with his mother again until he was thirteen. This rejection left him with insecurities that would follow him the rest of his life. "I know people [are] saying you're nothing and nobody and can never be anything," he would tell children when he was an adult. "I understand when you have no real last name . . . because our very genes cry out for confirmation."[2]

But Jesse's grandmother, Matilda "Tibby" Burns, was determined he was going to rise out of the poverty that had plagued his family since slavery. A maid in a white household, she would pick books and magazines out of the white family's garbage and give them to Jesse to read so he could better himself. "She never stopped dreaming for me," Jackson said years later.[3]

When Jesse was sixteen, Charles Jackson adopted him and gave him his last name. Jesse excelled in his studies and at sports. After graduating from high school in Greenville, he accepted a football scholarship to the University of Illinois in Urbana. During Christmas break 1959, he returned home and tried to use the Greenville Public Library to conduct research for one of his classes. He was turned away because the library was for whites only. Angry, he returned the next summer and organized a protest on the library steps. He and seven other

Jesse Jackson

students were arrested in a televised event. It was Jackson's first civil rights protest.

By the end of his freshman year at the University of Illinois, Jackson had become fed up with the racism the African-American students faced, so he transferred to North Carolina Agricultural and Technical College, a mostly black college in Greensboro, South Carolina. In 1961, he met Jacqueline Brown, a sociology major at the school, and they were married on New Year's Eve 1962. They had two daughters and three sons over the next twelve years.

In 1962, Jackson joined the college's campus chapter of the Congress of Racial Equality (CORE) and soon became a major part of that group's civil rights demonstrations. In May 1963, he realized that fighting for civil rights would become his life's work when he gave a powerful speech outside an abandoned polio hospital. The hospital was built to house 125 people, but was being used to hold 400 students arrested for demonstrating for civil rights. "[The speech] threw me into a whole new psychic pattern," he said in a *Time* magazine interview in 1970. "It became a commitment for life."[4]

Jackson graduated from North Carolina Agricultural and Technical College with a degree in sociology in 1964. He also secured a scholarship to Chicago Theological Seminary in Chicago, Illinois. Jackson had thought about becoming a minister since he was a teenager. In 1965, he went to Selma, Alabama, to participate in the civil rights march on

Birmingham. After the march, he joined Martin Luther King, Jr.'s organization, the Southern Christian Leadership Council (SCLC).

King appointed Jackson to establish a Chicago branch of Operation Breadbasket in 1966. Operation Breadbasket was an SCLC program that worked to obtain equal rights for African-American businesses and jobs for African-American workers. Under Jackson's leadership, Operation Breadbasket became a huge success, creating 5,000 new jobs for African Americans in four years.[5] By 1967, SCLC had expanded the program nationwide, and Jackson was a nationally known figure.

Six months before graduating, Jackson left seminary school to join King full-time (later he was ordained a Baptist minister). Jackson was one of the SCLC members with King when he was killed on April 4, 1968. Like many people in the United States, he felt the loss for years. "When Dr. King was murdered in Memphis, we lost a great prophet who had done much to bring democracy within the reach of millions of blacks and other non-white and poor citizens," Jackson said in 1974.[6]

Jackson was viewed by many to be King's successor as leader of the civil rights movement. The attention given to Jackson by the news media caused friction within SCLC. In 1971, SCLC suspended him for sixty days because he independently organized a festival for black businesses. Jackson resigned from SCLC and formed his own organization,

Operation PUSH (People United to Save Humanity, later called People United to Serve Humanity). The goal of Operation PUSH was to help people of all races obtain meaningful, good-paying jobs.[7]

Jackson continued to lead demonstrations in Chicago throughout the early 1970s. He promoted a strike of African-American bus drivers and later protested against the exclusion of African Americans from city construction projects. "Blacks are at the bottom and they want freedom," he said. "They're saying in one sense, we want to be recognized. They're saying, let my people go! And that's a *demand*, not a request!"[8]

In the late 1970s, Jackson began touring inner-city schools to teach children about self-respect and self-reliance. The tours evolved into PUSH for Excellence, a branch of Operation PUSH. By the end of the decade, Jackson had emerged as virtually the sole national voice of the black community.[9] The time seemed ripe for him to enter politics. He decided to start at the top: president of the United States.

In 1984, Jackson ran for the Democratic nomination for president, campaigning on behalf of what he called a "rainbow coalition" of people of all races. That same year, he helped arrange for the release of an African-American soldier held prisoner in Lebanon and the release of twenty-two Americans held on drug charges in Cuba. Jackson did not receive the presidential nomination in 1984, but his speech at the Democratic convention in Atlantic

Jesse Jackson as a presidential candidate.

City, New Jersey, electrified all who heard it. "Our flag is red, white, and blue, but our nation is a rainbow—red, yellow, brown, black, and white, we are all precious in God's sight!" he declared.[10]

Jackson ran for president again in 1988, coming in a close second behind Michael Dukakis for the Democratic nomination. Jackson had once more lost the nomination, but he'd gained greater recognition. Not only was he the most widely recognized leader of black America, but his popularity had grown throughout the country.[11] More importantly, he had laid the groundwork for future generations of African Americans who aspired to national leadership. "I may not get there," he said at a meeting of SCLC the day after the 1988 convention, "but it is possible for our children to get there now."[12]

During the 1990s, Jackson continued to play an important role in politics and human rights. In 1991, during Operation Desert Shield, he arranged for the release of hostages in Iraq and Kuwait just before the start of the Persian Gulf War. In 1999, he participated in a demonstration to protest the shooting of an unarmed African street vendor in New York City and helped secure the release of three American soldiers captured by the Serbian army in the former Yugoslavia.

Throughout his life, Jesse Jackson has fought not only for African Americans, but for people of all races. "I am somebody!" he shouts, and not just for himself, but for all of America.[13]

Chapter Notes

Chapter 1. Charles Houston

1. Charles Hamilton Houston, "Don't Shout Too Soon," *Crisis*, March 1936, p. 79.

2. Genna Rae McNeil, *Groundwork: Charles Hamilton Houston and the Struggle for Civil Rights* (Philadelphia: University of Pennsylvania Press, 1983), p. 224.

3. Ibid., p. 42.

4. Mark V. Tushnet, *Making Civil Rights Law: Thurgood Marshall and the Supreme Court, 1936–1961* (New York: Oxford University Press, 1994), p. 7.

5. McNeil, p. 84.

6. Michael D. Davis and Hunter R. Clark, *Thurgood Marshall: Warrior at the Bar, Rebel on the Bench* (New York: Birch Lane Press, 1992), p. 55.

7. Juan Williams, *Eyes on the Prize: America's Civil Rights Years, 1954–1965* (New York: Viking, 1987), p. 11.

8. Mark Whitman, ed., *Removing a Badge of Slavery: The Record of Brown* v. *Board of Education* (Princeton, N.J.: Markus Wiener Publishing Inc., 1993), p. 20.

9. Williams, p. 35.

Chapter 2. Ella Baker

1. Darlene Clark Hine, ed., *Black Women in America* (Brooklyn, N.Y.: Carlson Publishing, 1993), p. 70.

2. Joanne Grant, *Ella Baker: Freedom Bound* (New York: John Wiley & Sons, 1998), p. 12.

3. Ibid., p. 34.

4. James Forman, *The Making of Black Revolutionaries* (Washington, D.C.: Open Hand Publishing, 1985), p. 404.

5. Hine, p. 72.

6. Grant, pp. 126–127.

7. Fred Powledge, *Free at Last? The Civil Rights Movement and the People Who Made It* (Boston: Little, Brown & Co., 1991), p. 228.

8. "Ella Baker: Lifetime Activist," *Essence*, February 1990, p. 49.

9. Juan Williams, *Eyes on the Prize: America's Civil Rights Years, 1954–1965* (New York: Viking, 1987), p. 137.

10. "Ella Baker: Lifetime Activist," p. 49.

11. Geraldine Wilson, "Essence Woman," *Essence*, May 1985, p. 38.

Chapter 3. Thurgood Marshall

1. Carl T. Rowan, *Dream Makers, Dream Breakers: The World of Justice Thurgood Marshall* (Boston: Little, Brown & Co., 1993), pp. 195–196.

2. Juan Williams, *Thurgood Marshall: American Revolutionary* (New York: Random House, 1998), pp. 25–26.

3. "The Law: The Tension of Change," *Time*, September 19, 1955, p. 26.

4. Michael D. Davis and Hunter R. Clark, *Thurgood Marshall: Warrior at the Bar, Rebel on the Bench* (New York: Birch Lane Press, 1992), p. 38.

5. Ibid., p. 90.

6. Mark V. Tushnet, *Brown v. Board of Education: The Battle for Integration* (New York: Franklin Watts, 1995), p. 84.

7. Ibid., p. 97.

8. Davis and Clark, pp. 177–178.

9. "The Law: The Tension of Change," p. 23.

10. Davis and Clark, p. 364.

11. Jacques Steinberg, "Marshall Is Remembered as More than a Justice," *The New York Times*, January 25, 1993, p. B10.

Chapter 4. Rosa Parks

1. Rosa Parks with Gregory J. Reed, *Quiet Strength: The Faith, the Hope, and the Heart of a Woman Who Changed a Nation* (Grand Rapids, Michigan: Zondervan Publishing House, 1994), p. 17.

2. Rosa Parks with Jim Haskins, *Rosa Parks: My Story* (New York: Dial Books, 1992), p. 15.

3. Ibid., pp. 108–109.

4. Rita Dove, "Rosa Parks: The Torchbearer," *Time*, June 14, 1999, pp. 166, 168.

5. "Double-Edged Blade," *Time*, January 16, 1956, p. 20.

6. Rosemary L. Bray, "Rosa Parks: A Legendary Moment, a Lifetime of Activism," *Ms.*, November/December 1995, p. 47.

7. "Congress Votes to Honor Rosa Parks with Gold Medal," *Jet*, May 10, 1999, p. 30.

8. Parks and Haskins, p. 183.

Chapter 5. Fannie Lou Hamer

1. Phyl Garland, "Negro heroines of Dixie play major role in challenging racist traditions," *Ebony*, August 1966, p. 28.

2. John Egerton, "Fannie Lou Hamer" (obituary), *Progressive*, May 1977, p. 7.

3. Garland, p. 29.

4. Kay Mills, *This Little Light of Mine: The Life of Fannie Lou Hamer* (New York: Penguin Group, 1993), p. 38.

5. Jerry DeMuth, "Tired of Being Sick and Tired," *The Nation*, June 1, 1964, p. 549.

6. Juan Williams, *Eyes on the Prize: American's Civil Rights Years, 1954–1965* (New York: Viking, 1987), p. 233.

7. Mills, p. 121.

8. E.W. Kenworthy, "Mississippi Factions Clash Before Convention Panel," August 23, 1964, in *Black Protest in the Sixties: Articles from The New York Times*, ed. by August Meier, Elliot Rudwick and John Bracey Jr. (New York: Marcus Wiener Publishing Inc., 1991), p. 92.

9. Mills, p. 263.

10. Eleanor Holmes Norton, "A Memory of Fannie Lou Hamer," *Ms.*, July 1977, p. 51.

Chapter 6. Malcolm X

1. David Gallen, ed., *Malcolm X as They Knew Him* (New York: Caroll and Graff Publishing, Inc., 1992), p. 186.

2. "X: The black martyred hero still haunts our consciousness. A new film burnishes the myth," *Newsweek*, November 16, 1992, p. 79.

3. Ibid.

4. Hans J. Massaquoi, "The Mystery of Malcolm X," *Ebony*, September 1964, p. 44.

5. Alex Haley with Malcolm X, *The Autobiography of Malcolm X* (New York: Ballantine Books, 1965), p. 38.

6. Ibid., p. 55.

7. "Malcolm's Brand X," *Newsweek*, March 23, 1964, p. 32.

8. Gertrude Samuels, "Feud Within the Black Muslims," *The New York Times Magazine*, March 22, 1964, p. 104.

9. Massaquoi, p. 40.

10. Haley, pp. 346–347.

11. Marshall Frady, "The Children of Malcolm," *The New Yorker*, October 12, 1992, p. 72.

12. "Death and Transfiguration, *Time*, March 5, 1965, p. 25.

13. "Violence versus Nonviolence," *Ebony*, April 1965, p. 168.

Chapter 7. Martin Luther King, Jr.

1. Martin Luther King, Jr., *A Testament of Hope: The Essential Writings of Martin Luther King, Jr.*, James M. Washington, ed. (San Francisco: Harper & Row, 1986), pp. 219–220.

2. David L. Lewis, *King: A Critical Biography* (New York: Praeger Publishers Inc., 1970), p. 16.

3. Martin Luther King, Jr., *The Autobiography of Martin Luther King, Jr.*, Clayborne Carson, ed. (New York: Warner Books Inc., 1998), p. 60.

4. Coretta Scott King, *Selections, The Martin Luther King, Jr., Companion: Quotations from the Speeches, Essays, and Books of Martin Luther King, Jr.* (New York: St. Martin's Press, 1993), p. 106.

5. Lewis, p. 98.

6. Martin Luther King, Jr., *A Testament of Hope*, p. 292.

7. Adam Fairclough, *Martin Luther King, Jr.* (Athens, Georgia: University of Georgia Press), p. 93.

8. Ibid., pp. 102–103.

9. Martin Luther King, Jr., *A Testament of Hope*, p. 286.

10. Alex Ayres, ed., *The Wisdom of Martin Luther King, Jr.* (New York: Meridian, 1993), p. 266.

Chapter 8. Andrew Young

1. Andrew Young, *An Easy Burden* (New York: HarperCollins, 1996), p. 23.

2. Andrew Young, *A Way Out of No Way* (Nashville: Thomas Nelson Publishers, 1994), p. 21.

3. Ibid., p. 33.

4. Young, *An Easy Burden*, p. 204.

5. "Young: Getting Out the Vote," *Newsweek*, September 6, 1976, p. 15.

6. Hamilton Bims, "A Southern Activist Goes to the House," *Ebony*, February 1973, p. 89.

7. Clayton Fritchey, "The Rise and Fall of Andy Young," *The Nation*, September 15, 1979, p. 201.

8. "Andrew Young Weds Carolyn McClain in Cape Town, S. Africa," *Jet*, April 15, 1996, p. 13.

9. Young, *An Easy Burden*, p. 474.

Chapter 9. Julian Bond

1. Julian Bond, introduction to *Eyes on the Prize: America's Civil Rights Years, 1954–1965* by Juan Williams (New York: Viking Penguin, 1987), pp. xi–xii.

2. Ibid., p. xii

3. Fred Powledge, *Free at Last? The Civil Rights Movement and the People Who Made It* (Boston: Little, Brown & Co., 1991), p. 111.

4. Claudia Dreifus, "The *Progressive* Interview: Julian Bond," *Progressive*, August 1998, p. 34.

5. Barbara Carlisle Bigelow, ed., *Contemporary Black Biography*, Vol. 2 (Gale Research Inc., Detroit, 1992), p. 24.

6. Powledge, p. 630.

7. "Two-time Loser," *Newsweek*, January 24, 1966, p. 29.

8. Ibid.

9. Simeon Booker, "Black Politics at the Crossroads," *Ebony*, October 1968, p. 42.

10. Ibid.

11. "Julian Bond Seeks Divorce After 27-Year Marriage," *Jet*, August 15, 1988, p. 12.

12. Jack E. White, "'It's Still White Supremacy': Julian Bond restores the focus of the NAACP," *Time*, July 27, 1998.

Chapter 10. Jesse Jackson

1. "Jesse Jackson: One Leader Among Many," *Time*, April 6, 1970, p. 16.

2. Marshall Frady, *Jesse: The Life and Pilgrimage of Jesse Jackson* (New York: Random House, 1996), p. 86.

3. Ibid., p. 81.

4. "Jesse Jackson: One Leader Among Many," p. 21.

5. Ibid., p. 15.

6. Jesse L. Jackson, "Completing the Agenda of Dr. King: Operation PUSH," *Ebony*, June 1974, p. 117.

7. "A Split in SCLC," *Newsweek*, Dec. 20, 1971, p. 28.

8. "A Dialogue on Separation: Chicago 'Country Preacher' and Harvard Psychiatrist Exchange Ideas," *Ebony*, Aug. 1970, p. 63.

9. Frady, pp. 294–296.

10. Ibid., p. 366.

11. Elizabeth O. Colton, *The Jackson Phenomenon: The Man, the Power, the Message* (New York: Doubleday, 1989), pp. 282–283.

12. Ibid., p. 279.

13. Ibid., p. 8.

Further Reading

Allen, Zita. *Black Women Leaders of the Civil Rights Movement*. Danbury, Connecticut: Franklin Watts, 1996.

Celsi, Teresa. *Rosa Parks and the Montgomery Bus Boycott*. Brookfield, Connecticut: Millbrook Press, 1991.

Dunn, John M. *The Civil Rights Movement*. San Diego: Lucent Books, 1998.

Hess, Debra. *Thurgood Marshall: The Fight for Equal Justice*. Englewood Cliffs, New Jersey: Silver Burdett Press, 1990.

Hunter, Nigel. *Martin Luther King, Jr*. New York: Bookwright Press, 1985.

Jordan, June. *Fannie Lou Hamer*. New York: Cromwell, 1972.

McKissack, Patricia C. *Jesse Jackson: A Biography*. New York: Scholastic, 1989.

Rediger, Pat. *Great African Americans in Civil Rights*. New York: Crabtree, 1996.

Roberts, Naurice. *Andrew Young, Freedom Fighter*. Chicago: Children's Press, 1983.

Stine, Megan. *The Story of Malcolm X, Civil Rights Leader*. New York: Dell Publishing, 1994.

Internet Addresses

Brown v. *Board of Education of Topeka* (Kansas)
<http://www.digisys.net/users/hootie/brown>

Malcolm X Research
<http://www.brothermalcolm.net>

Martin Luther King, Jr., Center
<http://www.thekingcenter.com>

Martin Luther King, Jr., Day on the Net
<http://www.holidays.net/mlk>

The National Civil Rights Museum
<http://www.midsouth.rr.com/civilrights>

National Women's Hall of Fame
<http://www.greatwomen.org>

Charles Houston Bar Association
<http://www.charleshouston.org>

National Association for the Advancement of Colored People
<http://www.naacp.org>

The Rosa and Raymond Park Institute for Self-Development
<http://www.rosaparks.org>

Rainbow/PUSH organization
<http://www.rainbowpush.org>

Index